PRESENT NOT PERFECT
for Teens

•·•·•·•·•·•·•·•·•·•·•·•·•·•·•·•·•·•·•·

A JOURNAL FOR SLOWING DOWN,
LETTING GO, AND BEING
YOUR AWESOME SELF

Aimee Chase,
AUTHOR OF *PRESENT, NOT PERFECT*

CASTLE POINT BOOKS
NEW YORK

www.stmartins.com
www.castlepointbooks.com

The Castle Point Books trademark is owned by Castle Point Publishing, LLC.
Castle Point books are published and distributed by St. Martin's Press.

ISBN 978-1-250-20232-1 (trade paperback)

Cover and interior design by Tara Long.

Images used under license from Shutterstock.com.

Our books may be purchased in bulk for promotional, educational,
or business use. Please contact your local bookseller or the Macmillan
Corporate and Premium Sales Department at 1-800-221-7945, extension 5442,
or by email at MacmillanSpecialMarkets@macmillan.com.

First Edition: March 2019

10 9 8 7 6 5 4 3 2 1

Teenagers who have been through severe trauma or suffer from mental
illness should ask a professional before doing some of the meditative
practices suggested in this book. This book is *not* meant to be used in place
of professional counseling or therapy.

THIS JOURNAL
BELONGS TO:

· ·

YOU ARE ENOUGH

INTRODUCTION

SOMETIMES BEING A TEENAGER is like walking an impossibly thin line between childhood and adulthood. Parents, friends, and teachers expect a lot from you, and you demand a whole lot from yourself.

Present, Not Perfect for Teens is a colorful and mindful escape from the frantic, competitive, judgmental forces that can make you feel like less than enough. This is your personal invitation to slow down, pay attention to what really matters, and reframe your thinking for extra positivity. Empowered with the tips and short exercises inside this journal, you can rise above the judgmental world of social media and the constant school-day drama and embrace a healthier, happier mind-set.

Have fun choosing from the thoughtful prompts and reflective exercises that follow. Laugh at yourself, celebrate yourself, forgive yourself, but most importantly, love and accept yourself. Being a teenager isn't easy, but it's a time of incredible thrills, growing freedom, and brand-new experiences. Try on a more mindful point of view and embrace your perfectly imperfect teenage life.

THE WORLD WITHIN ME

THERE IS A WHOLE WORLD INSIDE OF YOU;
A GALAXY THAT ONLY YOU UNDERSTAND. THE MORE YOU
VISIT THAT WORLD, THE BETTER YOU WILL KNOW YOURSELF.

TAKE TIME TO SIT IN STILLNESS TODAY and
consider what's going on inside of you. Draw how you
envision your inner world below:

FIND YOUR PEACE

BUNDLES OF EMOTION

EMOTIONS DON'T USUALLY COME ONE AT A TIME,
BUT RISE UP IN COMPLICATED AND CONFUSING BUNDLES.

What emotions get tangled up with others? Describe
a time when you felt many emotions bubbling up at once.

4

HOW DO YOU UNTANGLE YOUR FEELINGS?
How do you figure out which emotions
are hiding behind the others?

1. CHAT WITH A FRIEND

2. TALK TO A FAMILY MEMBER

3. POUR YOUR HEART OUT IN A JOURNAL

4.

5.

6.

7.

QUEEN OF NOW

IT'S EASY TO FOCUS ON WHAT WE WANT, INSTEAD OF
WHAT ALREADY MAKES US RICH.

What makes you feel grateful?

What are the **PRECIOUS GEMS** that
sparkle bright in your life right now?

Cloudy Thoughts

Are there any clouds hanging over you today?
If so, describe them below.

REMIND YOURSELF THAT CLOUDS COME AND GO,
BUT THE SKY REMAINS.

Is there a way that you can turn one of those worries or
NEGATIVE THOUGHTS INTO AN OPPORTUNITY
or a positive thing?

Getting a bad cold ➡

Reason to nap!
Possible day off
from school!

NOW YOU TRY!

➡

MAKE PEACE WITH YOUR MOOD TODAY.
GIVE YOURSELF PERMISSION AND TIME TO FEEL WHATEVER
IT IS YOU'RE FEELING. COLOR THESE CLOUDS IN ALL THE
HUES THAT REFLECT YOUR CURRENT EMOTIONS.

YOU'VE GOT THIS

SHADOWS OF DOUBT

TAKE A MOMENT TO CONSIDER A
TIME WHEN YOU DOUBTED YOURSELF.

Have you ever expected to fail or underestimated your ability?
Describe that time below.

What effect do you think your
doubts have on your life?

IF YOU CAN'T
TRUST YOURSELF...

ON A SCALE OF 1 TO 5 STARS, HOW MUCH DO YOU
TRUST YOURSELF TO MAKE THE DECISIONS BELOW? FILL IN THE STARS
TO SHOW HOW MUCH CREDIT YOU GIVE YOURSELF.

DECISIONS ABOUT FRIENDS

NOT AT ALL   COMPLETELY

DECISIONS ABOUT WHAT TO POST ON SOCIAL MEDIA

NOT AT ALL   COMPLETELY

DECISIONS ABOUT YOUR HEALTH

NOT AT ALL   COMPLETELY

DECISIONS ABOUT SCHOOLWORK

NOT AT ALL   COMPLETELY

DECISIONS ABOUT YOUR FUTURE

NOT AT ALL   COMPLETELY

WHAT KINDS OF DECISIONS DO YOU MAKE WITH THE MOST CONFIDENCE?
Why do you think that is?

When do you doubt yourself most? Why do you think that is?
Consider your successes in this area (take your time
to dig them up—they're there) and write them below.
Come back to this list when you begin to doubt yourself.

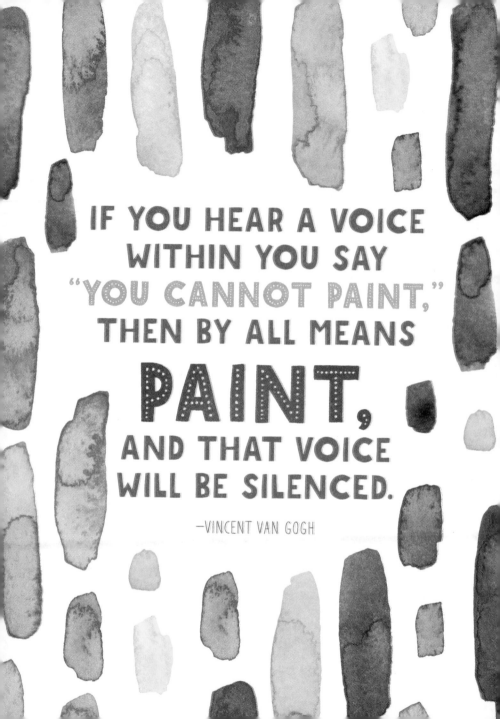

IF YOU HEAR A VOICE
WITHIN YOU SAY
"YOU CANNOT PAINT,"
THEN BY ALL MEANS
PAINT,
AND THAT VOICE
WILL BE SILENCED.

—VINCENT VAN GOGH

Doubt Detective

WHAT HAVE YOU TOLD YOURSELF YOU CANNOT DO?
WHAT HAVE YOU TOLD YOURSELF YOU ARE BAD AT DOING?
WRITE THESE DOUBTS BELOW:

Were these messages based on truth or fear of failure?
DRAW A BIG X through any of the above that you suspect
are more fiction than fact. Resolve to try them.

Cheerleader Brain

**THINK ABOUT THE CONVERSATIONS
THAT WENT ON INSIDE YOUR HEAD TODAY.**
WHEN YOU START TO PAY ATTENTION TO YOUR OWN INNER VOICE,
YOU WILL NOTICE THAT YOU CAN EITHER BE YOUR OWN
BEST CHEERLEADER OR YOUR OWN WORST ENEMY.

What encouraging words did you tell yourself today?

What negative messages did you give yourself today?

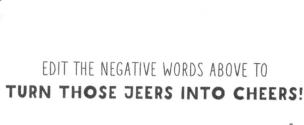

EDIT THE NEGATIVE WORDS ABOVE TO
TURN THOSE JEERS INTO CHEERS!

GOOD-ENOUGH DECISIONS

MAKING DECISIONS CAN BE REALLY STRESSFUL–
ESPECIALLY WHEN YOU BELIEVE THAT THERE IS ONLY
ONE RIGHT MOVE. MOST OF THE TIME, THERE IS NO CLEAR
OR PERFECT CHOICE. PUSH PAST THE DOUBTS, **TRUST
YOURSELF TO DO WHAT'S RIGHT FOR YOU,**
AND MAKE A CHOICE WITHOUT LOOKING BACK.

What decisions have been stressing you out lately?

Describe what you're afraid will
happen if you make the wrong choice:

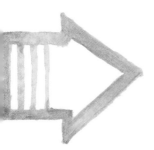

REMIND YOURSELF THAT **YOU CAN HANDLE
WHATEVER COMES YOUR WAY.**

TIME IS ON YOUR SIDE

What decision do you revisit wondering
if you made the right choice?

IMAGINE THE RIPPLES OF THAT DECISION
GETTING SMALLER AND MORE DISTANT AS TIME PASSES.

TRACE THE WAVES BELOW with your fingertip
as you release those choices into the past.

SLOW DOWN

BE AWARE OF THE PACE OF YOUR MIND AND BODY TODAY. Are your thoughts on the RIGHT NOW or the COMING SOON? Jot down all the times you notice yourself skipping ahead today instead of enjoying the present.

THE NEXT TIME ANXIETY IN THE FORM OF "WHAT'S NEXT" TAKES OVER, CATCH IT IN THE ACT—IF JUST FOR AN EXTRA SECOND—AND REMIND YOURSELF THAT LIFE IS NOT A RACE. TAKE A SLOW BREATH AND **BE THE HAPPY SLOTH HANGING FROM ITS BRANCH.** LINGER IN THE PRESENT AS IF THE PAST AND FUTURE DIDN'T EXIST.

High Alert!

THE NEXT TIME YOUR PHONE VIBRATES OR MAKES A SOUND CALLING
FOR YOUR ATTENTION, NOTICE HOW IT MAKES YOU FEEL.

CIRCLE THE WORD THAT
BEST DESCRIBES THAT FEELING:

ANXIOUS   INTERESTED   **LOVED**

EXCITED   HAPPY   SATISFIED

NEEDED   **NERVOUS**   ANNOYED

WHAT IF YOU CAN'T GET TO YOUR PHONE?
Does the feeling get stronger, change into
something else, or stay the same?

POWER DOWN

IMAGINE THAT YOUR CELL PHONE DROPPED
INTO A LAKE TODAY AND SANK TO THE BOTTOM. WHAT WOULD YOU
BE LOSING? WHAT WOULD YOU BE AFRAID WOULD HAPPEN?

What would you be free to do?

How could you free yourself in this way for
JUST A LITTLE BIT of time every day?

LOW NOTES

IT'S TEMPTING TO PULL AWAY FROM OTHERS WHEN YOU ARE SAD OR UPSET. WHILE IT'S OKAY TO WALLOW, **RESIST THE URGE TO BUILD A WALL AROUND YOURSELF.** USE MUSIC TO REMIND YOU THAT YOU'RE NOT ALONE IN YOUR FEELINGS.

List songs or lyrics below that speak to how you feel when times are tough:

When you're down, reach for songs and connections. **MAKE TIME TO PLAY MUSIC THAT SOOTHES YOU.** Observe the song's effect on your mind and body.

MUSIC
IS THE LANGUAGE
OF THE SPIRIT.

—KAHLIL GIBRAN

Practice Awareness

OBSERVING YOUR SURROUNDINGS IS
ONE EASY WAY TO ADD MEANING TO A MOMENT.

Look around you and find an object you're drawn to
(for any reason). **DRAW OR DESCRIBE** the object below
and what about it appeals to you.

Use this simple activity to connect to the present
when you're sitting in class, lounging at home,
or feeling rushed and stressed out.

HERE
AND
NOW

YOU, PAST AND PRESENT

Write down a few words to describe who you were
at each stage of your life and notice how together these
ages reflect the beautiful mosaic of your personality.

AS A BABY:

AS A TODDLER:

AS A GRADE SCHOOLER:

NOW:

What has stayed the same about you?

IMAGINE THAT THE SHAPES BELOW are your
unique, overlapping layers. Spend a quiet moment
appreciating all that you are in this moment.

BE TRUE

WE'RE ALL TEMPTED TO **ADD FLATTERING FILTERS** TO OUR PUBLIC LIVES.

Imagine that you could shed all of that pressure and all of those false layers and emerge as your true self. Who would you be and how would it feel?

Draw a self-portrait or add in a "normal you" photo. No filter. No glitter. **JUST YOU: RAW AND REAL.**

KNOWING YOURSELF IS THE BEGINNING OF ALL WISDOM.

—ARISTOTLE

Rainbow Zebra

COLOR IN THE ZEBRA AT LEFT ANY WAY YOU WANT
AND CONSIDER THE QUALITIES THAT MAKE YOU UNIQUE.

What do you like most about yourself?

Who loves you for all that you are?

Why is it great to be you?

WHY FIT IN WHEN YOU WERE
BORN TO STAND OUT?
—DR. SEUSS

MOMENTS TO REMEMBER

WITHOUT MINDFULNESS, YOU CAN WANDER
THROUGH A WHOLE DAY AS IF YOU ARE SLEEPWALKING.

Stop to take a snapshot of this moment in time
(YES, RIGHT NOW!) and consider how you're feeling.
Describe what you notice around you and within you.

CLICK!

What do you want to remember most about this moment?

What memories make you smile?

Why do you think these moments stay with you?

REVISIT YOUR BEST HIGHLIGHT REEL OF MEMORIES
WHEN YOU NEED TO ADD A SPRINKLE OF JOY TO YOUR "RIGHT NOW."

FIND **YOUR TRIBE**

HAVING A TRIBE OF **PEOPLE WHO ACCEPT YOU** CAN MAKE LIFE A LOT HAPPIER.

What kind of people do you like to surround yourself with?

When have you felt rejected by a friend?

How did you move past this feeling?

Who are your closest friends at school?

How do they live up to your tribe standards?

JUST BREATHE

SYNC YOUR MIND AND BODY

YOUR MIND CAN'T RELAX if your body isn't relaxed.
Try this quick meditative exercise to synchronize them.
Lie flat on your back on the grass or on a soft carpet. Take a few
minutes to do a mindful scan of your whole body from your feet
to the top of your head. On every exhale, move to a new part
of your body and make note of the physical sensations there.
Notice where you feel tense and relax those muscles as you go.
Describe how you feel before, during, and after this scan below:

BEFORE	DURING	AFTER

ENJOY THIS PEACEFUL CHECK-IN ANYTIME—
ESPECIALLY WHEN YOU FEEL OVERWHELMED OR STRESSED.

Lighten Your Load

CONSIDER YOUR DARKEST AND HEAVIEST THOUGHTS. WRITE THEM ON THE THE BALLOONS BELOW:

What if your fears amount to nothing; what if you are only wasting time by worrying? **IMAGINE THESE THOUGHTS LIGHTENING AND LIFTING HIGH INTO THE AIR** until they are completely out of sight. What would you be free to do without these thoughts weighing you down?

IF YOU HAVE
good thoughts
THEY WILL SHINE
OUT OF YOUR FACE
LIKE SUNBEAMS AND
YOU WILL ALWAYS
LOOK LOVELY.

—ROALD DAHL

A STEP IN THE RIGHT DIRECTION

AIMING FOR PERFECTION IN ALL AREAS OF YOUR LIFE CAN MAKE YOU FEEL LIKE YOU'RE NEVER DOING OR BEING ENOUGH. MAYBE IT'S OKAY IF YOU'RE JUST IN ONE SCHOOL CLUB FOR NOW, NOT FOUR. MAYBE BEING SUPER-ORGANIZED WOULD BE INCREDIBLE, BUT FOR NOW YOU'RE JUST GOING TO KEEP BETTER TRACK OF YOUR HOUSE KEY.

Write a **BIG GOAL** on the peak
of the tallest mountain below.

At the base of the mountain, write one step you
can take to move confidently toward your goal.

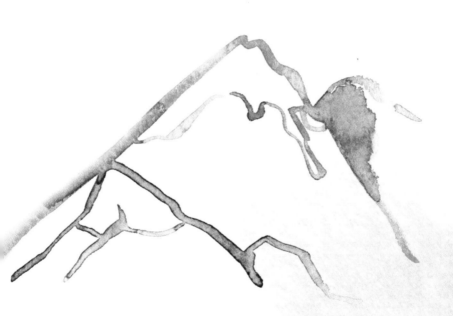

MAKE

THE

LEAP

DIVE IN

ACTING OUTSIDE OF YOUR COMFORT ZONE
IS ONE WAY TO WAKE YOURSELF UP TO YOUR POTENTIAL, REMIND YOU OF THE JOY OF LIFE, AND BUILD UP YOUR SELF-CONFIDENCE.

What bold moves have you made in your life?

WHAT HOLDS YOU BACK from making more moves like this?

What is your next big leap?

MINDFUL MORNINGS

USE A MORNING RITUAL TO HELP YOU FEEL MORE PRESENT TODAY. PRACTICE TURNING A MINDLESS ACTIVITY INTO A MINDFUL, SENSORY EXPERIENCE.

When you sip your hot cocoa or coffee, consider how the warmth of the mug feels on your fingertips. When you brush, how do the wet bristles feel against your teeth? What sound does the brushing make? If your mind wanders elsewhere, gently direct your thoughts back to the morning ritual.

DESCRIBE YOUR SENSORY EXPERIENCE HERE:

What rituals do you find most relaxing?
Circle some options below or add your own.

SIPPING A
HOT DRINK

TAKING
A SHOWER

DRIVING/WALKING
TO SCHOOL

MORNING
MUSIC

BRUSHING
YOUR TEETH

WASHING
YOUR HANDS

....

What rituals would you like to add to your life?

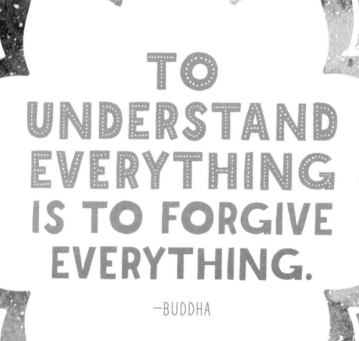

TO UNDERSTAND EVERYTHING IS TO FORGIVE EVERYTHING.

—BUDDHA

Loving an Imperfect World

GROWING UP MEANS NOTICING THE CRACKS AND FLAWS THAT EXIST IN PEOPLE AND IN THE REAL WORLD. ONE OF THE MOST FRUSTRATING THINGS TO LEARN IS THAT **ADULTS AREN'T PERFECT.**

What are some problems or hard truths you've discovered in the past few years? Write them between the jagged lines below.

NOTICE THE ONES YOU CAN WORK TO CHANGE.
LET THE OTHERS GO.

NAME THAT FEELING

If you had to define your mood today in terms of a color, which of these colors would you choose and why?

SOMETIMES JUST **ACKNOWLEDGING HOW YOU FEEL AND GIVING IT A NAME CAN MAKE YOU FEEL MORE CENTERED AND SELF-AWARE.** WE TEND TO THINK THAT THE EXTERNAL WORLD CAUSES OUR MOODS, BUT OFTEN IT IS JUST A CHANGE OF WEATHER THAT HAPPENS INSIDE OF US. NAMING YOUR EMOTION REMINDS YOU THAT WHAT YOU'RE FEELING IS TEMPORARY AND WILL PASS.

How would you define your current mood in words?

FIND YOUR
HAPPINESS FORMULA

WHAT ALWAYS SEEMS TO BOOST YOUR MOOD?
YouTube cat videos? A laugh with your best friend?
Going for a run? Write all of the happiness boosters
you can think of on the potion bottles at right.

USE THESE BOOSTERS WHEN YOUR SPIRIT
IS DOWN AND OUT. YOU CAN'T STOP TRAIN-WRECK DAYS
FROM HAPPENING, BUT YOU CAN ACKNOWLEDGE THEM
AND LEARN TO COPE WITH THEM MORE EASILY.

SACRED GROUND

THERE ARE SOME THINGS THAT MEAN MORE TO US THAN OTHERS WILL EVER KNOW: A CHILDHOOD PHOTO. AN OLD SWEATER. A TRINKET PASSED DOWN FROM GRANDPARENTS.

What objects are most meaningful to you?
List them in the shape below.

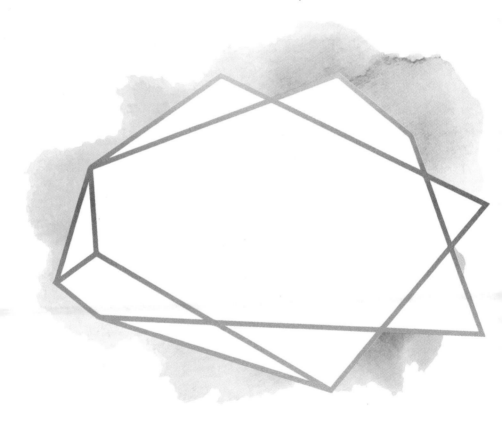

What places are most meaningful to you? They can be
a vacation spot, a cozy nook in your home, the forest,
or anywhere on Earth. List them below.

FIND TIME TO VISIT **PLACES THAT
MAKE YOU FEEL MOST AT PEACE.**

BE CAREFUL
HOW YOU
SPEAK TO
YOURSELF.
YOU ARE
LISTENING.

How I Love Me

WRITE A KIND AND CARING NOTE
TO YOURSELF IN THE SPACE BELOW. TELL YOURSELF
ALL OF THE WAYS IN WHICH YOU ARE AMAZING AND
MENTION ALL OF THE THINGS YOU ARE DOING RIGHT.

TASTING THE MOMENT

FOOD CAN GIVE US INSTANT PLEASURE AND WAKE US UP
TO THE MOMENT AT HAND. **USE FLAVORFUL FOODS TO
SAVOR THE MOMENT TODAY.** WHAT ARE
YOUR FAVORITE SENSORY-RICH TREATS? CIRCLE YOUR TOP PICKS
FROM THESE OPTIONS OR ADD YOUR OWN:

PEPPERMINT

CHOCOLATE

LEMONS

**HOT TEA
OR COFFEE**

ORANGES

SPICY FOOD

MINDFUL MEALS

TRY THIS MINDFULNESS CHALLENGE: **TREASURE THE FIRST THREE BITES OF EVERY FOOD YOU EAT TODAY.** ACT LIKE YOU'VE NEVER HAD THIS FOOD BEFORE IN YOUR LIFE. LET YOUR MOUTH NOTICE ITS UNIQUE TEXTURE, TEMPERATURE, AND FLAVOR. CONSIDER THE FEELINGS AND MEMORIES THIS FOOD INSPIRES. RECORD YOUR OBSERVATIONS HERE:

FOOD 1:

FOOD 2:

FOOD 3:

QUESTION
YOUR ANXIETY

THERE ARE EMOTIONS AND INSTINCTS YOU CAN TRUST, AND THEN THERE ARE THE ONES THAT LIE. ANXIETY IS ONE OF THOSE EMOTIONS. IT FEELS LIKE A KNOT THAT CAN'T BE UNRAVELED; A PROBLEM THAT CAN NEVER BE SOLVED; A FEAR YOU CAN'T FACE. CALL ITS BLUFF.

Unravel a current worry to its end. What would happen if something you've been anxious about actually happened?

Explain how you could handle it below:

STAY COOL

Let Me Be Me

LABELS ARE A REALITY OF TEEN LIFE.
EVERYONE WANTS TO DEFINE YOU AND
PUT YOU IN A BOX, BUT YOU DESERVE MORE.

What judgments (good or bad) do you
think people make about you?

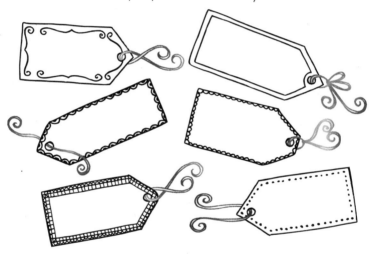

CROSS OUT THE LABELS ABOVE that
bother you most. Why do they bother you?

MAKE SOME JUDGMENTS
ABOUT YOURSELF BELOW:

I am a caring ....

I'm doing the best I can at ....

My strength is my ....

I'm becoming a better ....

I should be proud of myself for ....

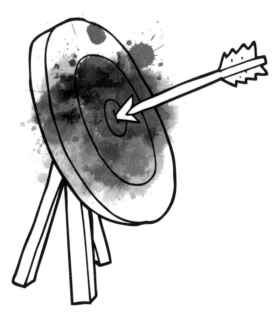

FINE-TUNING

SOUND IS A SIMPLE MEDITATION TOOL.

DOWNLOAD A MINDFULNESS BELL OR GONG AND PLAY IT AS YOU SIT
QUIETLY, FOCUSING ON NOTHING BUT THE SOUND. AS THE SOUND FADES
INTO OBLIVION, IMAGINE THAT YOUR STRESS IS DOING THE SAME.

Where did your thoughts go as you
waited for the sound to fade?

Which sounds put you most at ease?

GENTLE
HEARTBEAT

CLASSICAL
MUSIC

SOFT
SNORING

BIRDS SINGING

OCEAN
WAVES

RAIN

WIND CHIMES

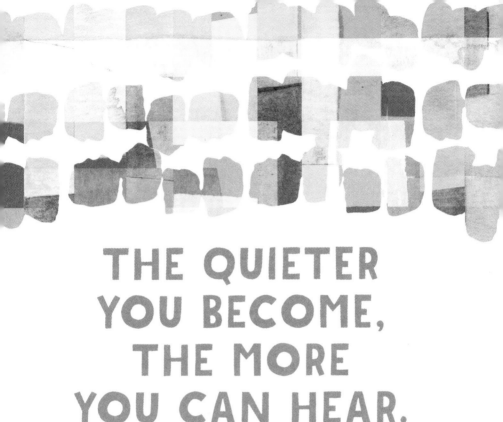

THE QUIETER YOU BECOME, THE MORE YOU CAN HEAR.

—RAM DASS

TRAVEL MUG HALF FULL

DO A QUICK CHECK-IN WITH YOURSELF
FROM TIME TO TIME TO SEE HOW YOU'RE FEELING.
DON'T JUDGE YOURSELF FOR YOUR ATTITUDE: REFLECT ON IT.

Color in the to-go cup below to reflect how positive your
thoughts are at the moment. Is the cup at least half full?

If your cup isn't completely full, CONSIDER ALL THE THINGS THE CUP ALREADY CONTAINS. Instead of wanting more, write down all that you have below. Is it enough?

GRATEFULNESS IS A HELPFUL CURE FOR (OR EVEN A DISTRACTION FROM) DISSATISFACTION. **NUDGE YOURSELF TOWARD A GRATEFUL STATE OF MIND WHEN YOU CAN.**

IT IS NOT HAPPINESS THAT MAKES US GRATEFUL, BUT GRATEFULNESS THAT MAKES US HAPPY.
—BROTHER DAVID STEINDL-RAST

FREE TO BE

Add to this list of perfectly imperfect things:

A LITTLE KID SINGING OFF-KEY

BEDHEAD

YOUR OLD TEDDY BEAR

....

....

....

....

....

Give yourself permission to be you today, in all of your imperfect glory. Imperfect is interesting, complicated, and natural.

Date: ....

Today I'm giving myself permission to mess up, fall apart, or need help. I don't always have to dress and act perfectly or say the right thing. I'm human and I'm learning as I go like everyone else.

I will stop obsessing over my imperfections and start honoring them as part of what makes me a real, growing person.

Signed,

....

Mantra in the Making

SOMETIMES THE EASIEST WAY TO EXPLAIN SOMETHING IS TO SAY WHAT IT ISN'T. **COME UP WITH YOUR OWN DEFINITION OF LIFE** BELOW AND USE IT AS YOUR MANTRA.

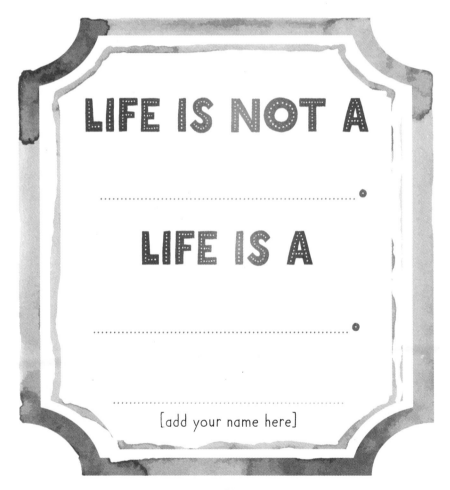

LIFE IS NOT A

....•

LIFE IS A

....•

....

[add your name here]

Describe or give an example of how you live by
(or want to live by) this philosophy.

DWELL ON THE
beauty of life.
WATCH THE STARS,
& see yourself
RUNNING
WITH THEM.

—MARCUS AURELIUS

LIVE LIKE A POET

DON'T LET A DAY GO BY WITHOUT NOTICING SOMETHING
BEAUTIFUL. MAKE A POINT TO **SEEK OUT THE SMALL,
EVERYDAY THINGS THAT MAKE LIFE MAGICAL.**
WHAT DID YOU SEE TODAY THAT INSPIRED YOU?

Write a short poem about it here:

BUSY MIND;
PEACEFUL SPIRIT

COLORING, KNITTING, PAINTING, AND DRAWING ARE JUST SOME OF THE **SOOTHING ACTIVITIES THAT OCCUPY THE LOGICAL AND CREATIVE PARTS OF OUR BRAIN** SO THAT THE PART THAT MANAGES EMOTION AND STRESS CAN DO ITS JOB BETTER. WHAT ACTIVITIES MAKE YOU FORGET YOUR WORRIES AND LIVE MORE IN THE MOMENT?

Consider how you feel in this moment. Take a short break to color the image at right or doodle in the margins of this page. Were you able to relax and tap into your inner world?

LIVE **LOUD**

SEIZE THE MOMENT AND SPEAK YOUR MIND TODAY. **THINK OF A TRUTH ABOUT YOURSELF** OR LIFE IN GENERAL THAT YOU'D LIKE TO OFFER TO THE WORLD. WRITE IT BELOW.

Open up a window and shout it as loud as you can. **EMBARRASSING? MAYBE.** But fun and liberating, too!

Does a quieter approach suit you better? What would you like to whisper to the world or to another person today?

Use the directions below to **MAKE AIRMAIL THAT LETS YOUR FEELINGS FLY.** Write the words you need to say on a paper airplane and launch your message for someone else to find.

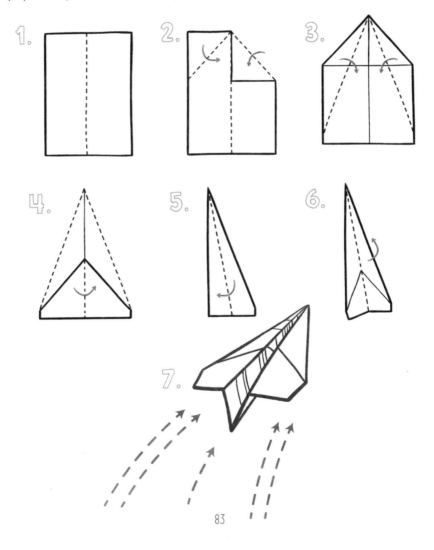

Beast Mode

LOOK TO ANIMALS WHEN YOU NEED INSPIRATION FOR LIVING A MINDFUL LIFE. ANIMALS DON'T STOP TO THINK ABOUT WHAT IT IS TO BE AN ANIMAL. **THEY SIMPLY EXIST AS THEY WERE MEANT TO EXIST** WITHOUT SEARCHING FOR MEANING.

Imagine that you could transform into your spirit animal today. **WHICH CREATURE WOULD YOU BECOME AND WHY?** How would it free you?

"TRANSFORM" INTO THE **MIND-SET OF YOUR SPIRIT ANIMAL** WHENEVER YOU NEED A BREAK FROM OVERTHINKING THINGS.

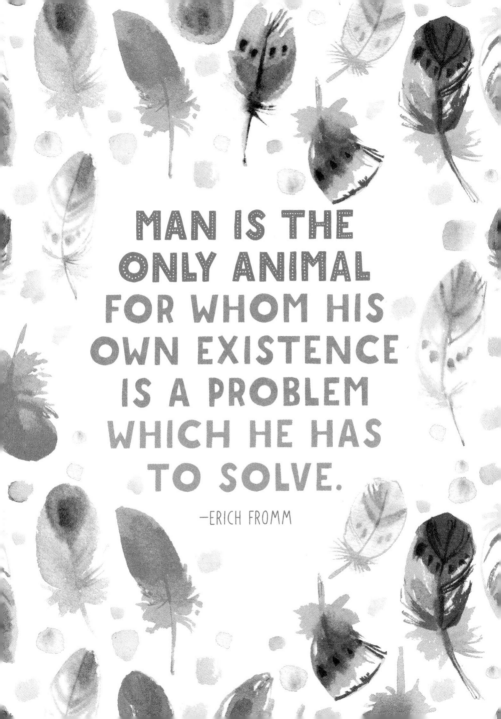

MAN IS THE ONLY ANIMAL FOR WHOM HIS OWN EXISTENCE IS A PROBLEM WHICH HE HAS TO SOLVE.

—ERICH FROMM

CLEAR THE SKY

TRY THIS MINDFUL MEDITATION FOR JUST A FEW MINUTES TO HELP YOU FEEL CENTERED AND AT PEACE.

Sit tall in a chair with your hands palms-down on your thighs or palms-up touching your thumb to your index finger.
Close your eyes and imagine that your mind is a clear, blue sky.
IF A THOUGHT POPS INTO THE SKY, LET IT FLITTER ACROSS LIKE A BIRD. Breathe naturally and focus on the sound of your breath. Notice the way the wind of your breath quiets to a gentle breeze.

DESCRIBE YOUR EXPERIENCE MEDITATING HERE.
How did you feel before, during, and after? What thoughts flittered across your sky while you meditated?

TRY DIFFERENT BODY POSITIONS for this same meditation exercise. Which one is most comfortable for you?

KNEELING

SITTING

LYING FLAT

....

[add your own]

REACH WITH YOUR HEART

BEING GENEROUS AND KIND TO OTHERS CAN REALLY LIFT OUR SPIRITS AND HEAL OUR HEARTS. **WHAT IS ONE GOOD DEED** YOU COULD DO TODAY TO REACH OUT WITH LOVE? ADD TO THE LIST BELOW:

- [ ] **SEND AN ENCOURAGING TEXT TO A FRIEND OR FAMILY MEMBER**
- [ ] **DONATE TO A CHARITY THAT MEANS A LOT TO YOU**
- [ ] **HUG SOMEONE WHO NEEDS IT**
- [ ] **THINK OF SOMEONE WHO ISN'T VERY KIND TO YOU. WISH THEM HAPPINESS.**
- [ ]
- [ ]
- [ ]

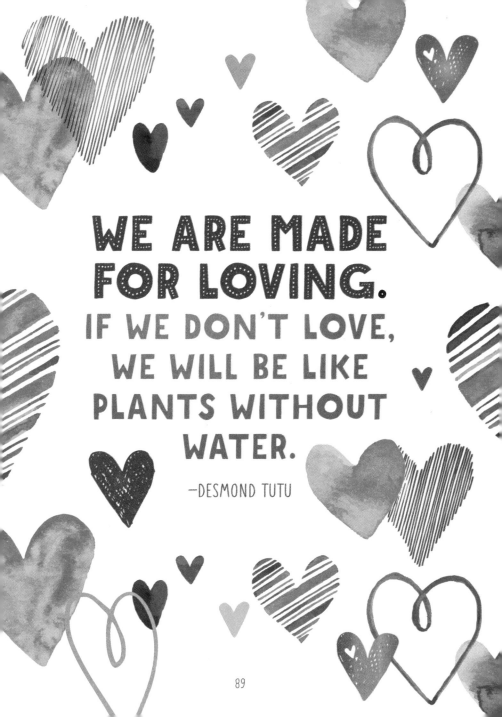

WE ARE MADE
FOR LOVING.
IF WE DON'T LOVE,
WE WILL BE LIKE
PLANTS WITHOUT
WATER.

—DESMOND TUTU

BRANCH OUT

TAKE TIME TO COMMUNE WITH NATURE TODAY.
WHETHER IT'S STARGAZING, WALKING IN THE WOODS,
OR PUDDLE JUMPING IN THE RAIN, GET SOME FRESH AIR
AND NATURAL WONDER AS OFTEN AS YOU CAN.

When was the last time you played outside?

How do you like to spend your time outdoors?

ADOPT THE PACE OF NATURE.

Her secret is patience.

—RALPH WALDO EMERSON

Winds of Change

CONNECTING WITH FAMILY IS ONE WAY TO FEEL GROUNDED, SAFE, AND SECURE, BUT YOU MAY HAVE TO DRIFT AWAY FROM FAMILY AS YOU LEARN TO CAPTAIN YOUR OWN SHIP. HOW HAVE YOUR FAMILY RELATIONSHIPS CHANGED AS YOU'VE GROWN?

With whom in your family do you have the easiest connection?

With whom in your family do you struggle to connect?
How might this struggle be rooted in love or changing needs?

SUPREME TEEN

THIS IS AN EPIC MOMENT IN YOUR LIFE,
THOUGH IT MAY NOT ALWAYS BE A PERFECT ONE. TAKE A
MOMENT TO REFLECT ON THE JOYS OF BEING A TEENAGER.
WHAT DO YOU LOVE MOST ABOUT THIS STAGE OF YOUR LIFE?

What experiences do you want to remember forever?

What do you miss about being a little kid?

What do you look forward
to about being an adult?

THIS I BELIEVE

EVERYONE NEEDS TO BELIEVE IN SOMETHING.
WRITE YOUR CORE VALUES AND DEEPEST TRUTHS
ON THE PETALS OF THIS LOTUS.

| HIGHER POWER | MYSELF | CHARITY |
| FAMILY | LOVE | WORLD PEACE |

Consider all that you have learned in your life already.
Write a few life lessons you've picked up below.

What answers are you still searching for?

THE THREE KEYS

THERE ARE THREE FACTORS, ACCORDING TO A RECENT STUDY,* THAT DETERMINE HOW HAPPY PEOPLE CAN BE: THEIR ABILITY TO TAKE PLEASURE IN THE SMALL THINGS, HOW MUCH THEY USE THEIR PERSONAL SKILLS, AND HOW MUCH THEY HELP OTHERS.

HOW WOULD YOU RATE YOURSELF IN THESE THREE AREAS OF YOUR LIFE, and what could you do to expand them? Write notes to yourself on the Venn diagram at right.

PLEASURE (IN SMALL THINGS)

1   2   3   4   5   6   7   8   9   10

ENGAGEMENT (OF SKILLS)

1   2   3   4   5   6   7   8   9   10

MEANING (THROUGH CHARITY)

1   2   3   4   5   6   7   8   9   10

KEYS TO HAPPINESS

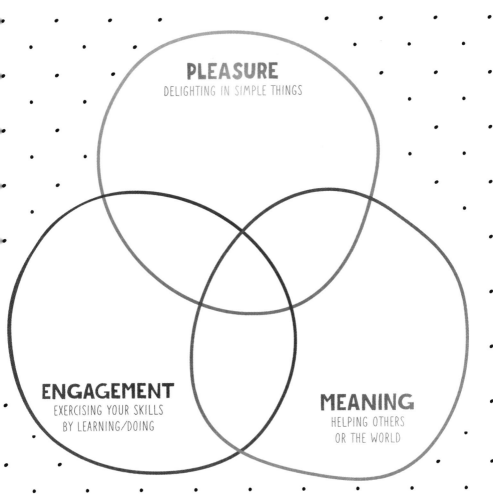

PLEASURE
DELIGHTING IN SIMPLE THINGS

ENGAGEMENT
EXERCISING YOUR SKILLS
BY LEARNING/DOING

MEANING
HELPING OTHERS
OR THE WORLD

*Schueller, Stephen, and Martin Seligman. "Pursuit of Pleasure, Engagement,
and Meaning: Relationships to Subjective and Objective Measures of Well-Being."
The Journal of Positive Psychology 5 (2010): 253–263.

CONFIDENCE IS
YOUR SUPERPOWER

WE ALL DOUBT OURSELVES AT TIMES; SOME OF US ARE JUST BETTER AT HIDING IT. **CARRYING YOURSELF WITH CONFIDENCE** (EVEN IF YOU HAVE TO FAKE IT AT FIRST) IS THE SIMPLEST ADVANTAGE YOU CAN GIVE YOURSELF. IT DOESN'T REQUIRE A HISTORY OF SUCCESS, JUST A DETERMINATION TO BELIEVE THAT YOU CAN DO IT.

Who are the most confident people you know?
What could you learn from them?

What are some courageous things you'd like to do or say?

ADD A DRAWING OR PHOTO OF YOURSELF ON THE COMIC BOOK COVER AT RIGHT.
COME BACK TO THIS PAGE WHEN YOU NEED TO TRANSFORM INTO CONFIDENT, SUPERHERO MODE TO FACE A CHALLENGE.

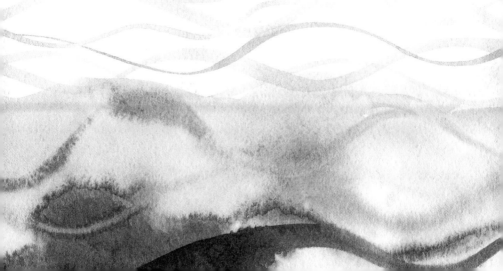
GO
WITH THE
FLOW

Free Your Mind

LET THE RIVER **OF YOUR** THOUGHTS
FLOW THROUGH YOUR PEN TODAY.

WRITE A STREAM-**OF**-CONSCIOUSNESS JOURNAL
ENTRY BELOW. Don't let any judgments about what you're
writing stop the flow. Just enjoy the act of setting loose
the untamed contents of your mind.

HEART SONG

LISTEN TO YOUR HEART'S QUIET SONG TODAY.
SIT CROSS-LEGGED OR KNEEL ON THE FLOOR WITH A HAND ON YOUR
CHEST AND FOCUS ON THE GENTLE THUD OF YOUR HEARTBEAT.
THINK OF ALL THE LOVE IN YOUR LIFE: LOVE FROM YOURSELF,
LOVE FROM YOUR FAMILY AND FRIENDS, LOVE FROM THE UNIVERSE.
IMAGINE THAT YOUR HEART IS POWERED BY THAT LOVE.

When do you feel most loved?

LOVE IS WHAT KEEPS US GOING
no matter what obstacles we face. Knowing how to
love and be loved is the greatest lesson of our lives.
Describe all the reasons you deserve love:

How can you add more love to your life or the lives of others?

What about love isn't perfect? What about it is scary?

What loves are you grateful to have or have had?

WHEN YOU REALIZE NOTHING IS LACKING, THE WHOLE WORLD BELONGS TO YOU.

—LAO TZU